# MOVING ON UP!

## MOLLY POTTER

This book is dedicated to Maddy Kirkham who is about to embark upon such a journey...

Published 2009 by A & C Black Publishers Ltd
36 Soho Square, London W1D 3QY

ISBN 978-1-4081-0913-7

Written by Molly Potter
Design by Cathy Tincknell
Illustration by Mike Phillips

Copyright © Molly Potter 2009

All rights reserved. This book may be photocopied for use in the school or educational establishment for which it was purchased, but may not be reproduced in any other form or by any other means – graphic, electronic or mechanical, including recording, taping or information retrieval systems – without the prior permission in writing of the publishers.

Printed in Great Britain by Martins the Printers, Berwick-on-Tweed

This book is produced using paper that is made from wood grown in managed, sustainable forests. It is natural, renewable and recyclable. The logging and manufacturing processes conform to the environmental regulations of the country of origin.

To see our full range of books visit
www.acblack.com

# Contents

| | |
|---|---|
| Introduction | 4 |
| Helping with transition | 5-9 |
| Teachers' notes | 10-15 |

## Photocopiable activities

### Dealing With Change
| | |
|---|---|
| Coping with change | 16 |
| What about change? | 17 |

### Changing Relationships
| | |
|---|---|
| The effects of peer pressure and influence | 18 |
| Peer influence – being 'cool' | 19 |
| Advice about peer pressure and influence | 20 |

### Help and Support
| | |
|---|---|
| What to do when you need help | 21 |
| Who would you turn to? | 22 |
| Anti-bullying | 23 |

### Moving On Up
| | |
|---|---|
| Going to secondary school – how do I feel? | 24 |
| Feelings about secondary school | 25 |
| Getting to know your new teachers | 26 |
| Secondary school freeze-frames | 27 |
| Transition quiz | 28 |
| Some information for my secondary school teachers | 29 |
| Turn over a new leaf | 30 |
| A letter to yourself | 31 |
| What do the pupils at secondary school say? | 32 |
| How organised are you? | 33 |
| Road traffic accidents | 34 |
| To secondary school I go! | 35-36 |

## Photocopiable Leaflets    37

| | |
|---|---|
| Moving on up – a leaflets for parents/carers | 38-39 |
| A big change? – a leaflet for pupils | 40-41 |
| Getting help and support – a leaflet for pupils | 42-43 |
| Changing relationships – a leaflet for pupils | 44-45 |
| Anti-bullying – a leaflet for pupils | 46-47 |

| | |
|---|---|
| Transition – is it a big deal? | 48 |

# Introduction

Moving up to secondary school is a pretty significant change that children have to go through. When you consider that it also happens at a time when many children are experiencing puberty, they are dealing with a huge amount of change in a relatively small amount of time. Such change without support is a lot to ask of children and it is no wonder that academic standards often plateau for some time after the transition to secondary school.

In sessions carried out with primary school children about moving to secondary school, the anticipation of getting lost, being overloaded with homework and bullying always dominated the discussions. It is great for the pupils to have a realistic expectation of some degree of unsettledness during transition but this can be mitigated with the idea that moving to a new school can be exciting, interesting and a chance to turn over a new leaf!

## Why use this book?

*Moving On Up!* aims to help pupils with the process of transition. It does this by providing teachers with a selection of ideas, activities and leaflets covering the topic of moving to secondary school – and the changes it brings – to use with their pupils. This book addresses:
- Coping with change
- The actual changes experienced before, during and after transition
- Changing relationships
- Skills needed to cope with changing relationships

## How can this book be used?

Many primary schools devote the PSCHE lessons in the last half of the summer term for their top year group to transition. However, preparations for transition usually begin far in advance of this half term (e.g. selecting which secondary school to attend, open days at the secondary schools, information about pupils being transferred etc.). This book provides a range of ideas and activities that can be used to support all stages of the process.

This book is split into five sections:

HELPING WITH TRANSITION
This gives practical ideas that can start to be implemented long before any PSCHE lessons on transition are delivered – particularly when liaising with the secondary school/s your pupils might be moving on to.

TEACHERS' NOTES
This gives guidance for each photocopiable activity sheet.

PHOTOCOPIABLE ACTIVITY SHEETS FOR PUPILS
These can be used to address the issues of transition to secondary school during primary school PSCHE lessons. These would most commonly happen in the last half term of the pupils' final year of primary school – while the topic is likely to be very much at the forefront of their minds. However, some of the activities (particularly those from the sections 'Dealing with change', 'Changing relationships' and 'Help and support') could be scattered throughout pupils' final primary school year as part of the general preparation for transition.

PHOTOCOPIABLE LEAFLETS FOR PARENTS/CARERS AND PUPILS
Each pair of pages can be photocopied back-to-back and folded to create leaflets to help inform parents/carers and pupils about the practical and emotional aspects of moving to secondary school. However, they could also be used by parents/carers as tools for prompting discussions with their child on these topics. Some of the activities in this book could be set as homework for this purpose too.

TRANSITION – IS IT A BIG DEAL?
Some final thoughts for all those involved in the transition process.

## Using the CD-ROM

The enclosed CD-ROM contains printable versions of all the activity sheets, as well as customisable versions of the activity sheets on pages 16-19, 21-23, 25, 27, 30 and 31. This means that teachers can customise these activities to address specific issues faced by their pupils during transition. For further information about the CD-ROM, please see the inside front cover.

# Helping with transition

The transition process and the effort made to help pupils transfer varies from school to school. This section provides you with ideas that could be used to help pupils prepare for and settle into secondary school.

## Gathering information from the secondary school/s

Much anxiety can be caused by parents/carers and pupils not knowing certain details about the secondary school they are due to go to. If the following information is collected from your local secondary school/s and shared with parents/carers and pupils it can help to alleviate this anxiety and can even have an impact on their decision about which school to attend (if there is a choice).

Many secondary schools have a member or members of staff that have been allocated the responsibility of liaising on matters to do with transition. Their involvement and commitment will vary but they are likely to be happy to respond to a request for information.

Possible information might include:

### SCHOOL PROCEDURES

#### HOW ARE PARENTS/CARERS KEPT INFORMED?
- How does the school keep parents/carers informed about school information and procedures?
- What procedures are in place for parents/carers to communicate with the school?

#### PASTORAL SUPPORT FOR PUPILS
- What systems exist in the school for supporting pupils with any worries or concerns they might have?
- Where do pupils get non-academic information and support from?

#### SPECIFIC INFORMATION
- If any pupils have specific needs (academic, health or personal) how is this information passed up to secondary school and who knows about it?

#### SUPPORTING NEW PUPILS
- What procedures does the school have in place to support pupils that have newly arrived at the school? e.g. mentors, welcoming activities in the first week, an induction programme?

#### ANTI-BULLYING
- What are the anti-bullying procedures in the school?
- How are pupils made aware of what to do if they encounter bullying?

### THE SCHOOL DAY

#### JOURNEY TO AND FROM SCHOOL
- If pupils travel to and from school by bus, cycle or are dropped off by car, is there any specific information they need to know?

#### REGISTRATION
- Where will pupils go when they arrive on the first day?
- What happens at registration?
- What else happens with the form/tutor or registration group?

TIMETABLE
- What will the timetable look like?
- How long are lessons, break and lunch times?
- What time does the day start and finish?

STORAGE OF PERSONAL ITEMS
- Do pupils have a place to store personal possessions e.g. a locker?

FINDING YOUR WAY AROUND
- What efforts does the school make to help new pupils find their way around the school e.g. maps, allowance for lateness in the first few weeks?

SCHOOL CLUBS
- What extra-curricular activities does the school offer?

IN THE CLASSROOM

CURRICULUM
- Are there any new subjects that pupils will have at secondary school that they did not have at primary? (e.g. a new modern foreign language, drama, metalwork, woodwork – as part of D&T, science split into biology, physics and chemistry etc.)

HOMEWORK
- Approximately how much homework can pupils expect each week from each subject area?
- What happens if a pupil has difficulty completing homework tasks?

GROUPING
- How will pupils be grouped for different subjects?
- Will pupils spend the majority of time in the same group or be jumbled up in every lesson?
- Will pupils be grouped with some of their friends from primary school?

SPECIFIC EQUIPMENT NEEDED
- What will pupils need to bring to school each day? (e.g. writing materials)
- What are the uniform and PE kit requirements of the school?
- What lunch facilities does the school offer? (e.g. is there a canteen? What are the prices?)
- What provision is made for packed lunches?

# An evening for parents/carers

Many primary and/or secondary schools have evening or afternoon sessions for the parents/carers of pupils that are about to go to secondary school. Some parents/carers understandably get quite anxious about their child's transition to secondary school. This can sometimes be because they found their own move up to secondary school a negative experience. Therefore, in such a session, you might aim to:
- Ensure parents/carers receive all the practical information they need.
- Reassure parents/carers that efforts are being made to attempt to make transition as smooth as possible for their children.
- Get plenty of opportunity for parents/carers to ask questions (not just in a large group as some parents/carers will find this intimidating).
- Disseminate leaflets (like those in the back of this book).

# Open days

Many secondary schools offer open or induction days to pupils that are about to leave primary school. The overall purpose of these days is usually to help pupils feel more positive about transition. These days might include activities that:

- Help pupils to orientate themselves in the new school building/s.
- Introduce school staff to the pupils.
- Give pupils generic information (such as that in the table on the previous pages).
- Give pupils a taster lesson to alleviate some fears they might have about the curriculum.
- Introduce current secondary pupils who will be acting as mentors for new pupils.
- Answer any questions pupils might have.
- Meet pupils from other primary schools who will also be attending the school.

Each secondary school will already have activities that are used to welcome prospective pupils. However, if strong links between primary and secondary schools have been made, open days could be planned by teachers from both/all schools. Here are some ideas that could be used as part of an open day.

## True or false?

Several secondary school teachers or one key member of staff (e.g. the new year group leader) could volunteer information about themselves. Some of this information could be true and some of it false. The information could be summarised in written form and given to the pupils. Pupils are then encouraged to ask more questions (the teacher can lie though) to help them ascertain which information is true and which is false. The information might include things such as:

- Middle or nicknames.
- Where they are from.
- Their family.
- Musical instruments they play.
- Languages they can speak.
- The lesson they hated most at school.
- Embarrassing moments.
- What they like about people.
- Favourite food/drinks/TV programmes/colour/leisure activity etc.

## Scavenger hunt

If primary school pupils get the opportunity to be in their new school while the rest of the school is not present, pupils could complete a scavenger hunt in the empty building to help them orientate themselves. They do not need to actually gather each thing – just find it and perhaps draw it or describe where it is. Examples of the kind of things they could hunt for include:

- A sign in a corridor that tells you not to do something.
- The name of a pupil who has work displayed in an English classroom.
- The colour of the chairs in the dining hall.
- The name of one of the secondary teacher's pets.
- A picture you have drawn of a piece of science equipment.
- A list of all the sports for which trophies have been won that are displayed in the foyer.

## Fact finding

Pupils can be given one of the following topics (or topics like them) and asked to find out as much as they can about each of the topics in three minutes by asking a member of staff questions that can be answered only with a yes or no ('difficult to answer' is a response you might also like to have). It is a good idea to give pupils planning time to consider the questions they are going to ask.

- Homework.
- How lessons are different.
- What is the same as at primary school?
- Where to get help.
- Pupils can then draw a poster that represents all they found out.

## Sample lessons

Many secondary schools deliver sample lessons to primary school pupils. These can be from any area of the curriculum but are often either science or P.E.

Alternatively staff might prefer to set all pupils the challenge of producing a skit that exaggerates their worst fears about lessons at secondary schools (e.g. really strict teachers, really difficult work, lots of homework being set, not knowing any of the other pupils, other pupils finding it easy when you find it really difficult... etc.). These fears could then be challenged!

## Question and answer session

Existing secondary pupils can sit on a panel and answer pre-prepared questions that the primary school pupils would like to ask them.

## Presentation from existing secondary school pupils

Secondary pupils give a presentation that sums up their experience of transition and that highlights the positive aspects of going to secondary school.

## Photo hunt

This activity can be used to help pupils orientate themselves in the new buildings. It is better if pupils can complete this in the absence of current secondary school pupils.
Photos need to have been taken from various positions throughout the school. Each photo is labelled with a letter and pupils need to mark the letter and an arrow from the letter on a map of the school to show where they think the photo was taken from and which direction the camera was pointing. It helps to give one example already completed on the map.

## Welcome leaflets

Secondary pupils can design and make welcome leaflets for the new pupil intake in advance of the open days. These leaflets could include information about:
- Settling in – how quickly does it happen and what helps.
- Where to get help.
- Secondary and primary schools – similarities and differences.
- The great things about secondary school.

The secondary pupils could hand their leaflets over to the primary school pupils, introduce themselves and answer questions about their leaflets.

## Getting to know you

This is a game for helping pupils from different primary schools to get to know each other.

Ask pupils to order themselves in a line:
- With their first names in alphabetical order.
- In birthday order.
- In height order.
- In distance they live from the school order.
- In length of arm order.
- In order from the person who most likes maths to least likes it.
- In order from the lightest hair colour to the darkest.
- In order from who can jump the furthest from standing to the least!
- In order from the person who has the most different colours on their clothing to the least... etc.

Obviously anyone who has the same characteristic needs to stand next to each other.

## Making friends

This helps pupils consider the challenge of meeting lots of new people and how best to make new friends.

Ask pupils to work in teams of three. If pupils from more than one primary school are present, aim for a mix of pupils from different schools in each team. Set each team the following challenge:

You are going to name, design and present the world's worst friend maker. It is up to you how you present your idea: a poster, a short play, an advert, a labelled diagram, the top ten tips they might write, a list of their behaviours, a newspaper report... etc.

After the presentations, discuss what helps people to make friends and consider the opposite of what they designed (the world's best friend maker).

## Other team challenges to help pupils get to know each other...

- Make a magical 'going to secondary school' survival kit (e.g. making-new-friend dust, homework wand, new-route-finder... etc.).
- Turn a map of the secondary school into some kind of a puzzle (e.g. a jigsaw, match the edges with the same symbols to reform a map that has been cut up, draw a route on the map responding to clues (this route could make a letter), guess the room by asking questions that can only be answered with a yes or no).
- Collect and present factual information about members of staff in an interesting way.
- Make the longest list you can of things you would like to happen to you on the first day at secondary school.
- Draw a poster that illustrates the main differences between primary and secondary school.

# Teacher's Notes

## Coping with change (p16)

PURPOSE OF ACTIVITY: to consider what makes a change something we look forward to, what makes it a big deal or not and what helps people to cope with change.

KEY DISCUSSION POINTS:

- Dreading or looking forward to a change depends on our perception of whether the change will be beneficial to us or not and how much control we feel we have over it. Sometimes change delivers us things we were not expecting (both positively and negatively)!
- Anticipating change with dread often means that when the time arrives, the change is not as bad as we thought.
- Really looking forward to a change can sometimes make the actual change a bit of a letdown!
- A change is a big one if it has a noticeable impact on our day-to-day existence so that we face lots of new ways of doing things and if it is permanent. A change can also be a big one if it makes us feel a strong emotion.
- Change can make our lives more adventurous. If a person tried to avoid all changes they would lead a very dull life. Change is also good for meeting people's needs at different times in their lives. For example, you would not want to be at nursery school until you were 16.
- Some people embrace change more than others. How much we do this depends on our basic personality and how secure we are made to feel when a change is implemented.
- Advice about coping with change might include:
  - remember change is good for learning new things
  - consider how dull life would be without change
  - find out as much information as you can, as not knowing things can make you feel more uncertain about change
  - talk through any worries about change with someone you trust
  - a change might make you feel unsure for a short time but you'll soon be back on track... etc.

EXTENSION ACTIVITIES

- Pupils could do a short skit that contrasts a positive and a negative approach to change.
- Pupils could make a poster of the top five tips to help someone deal with change.
- Pupils could write a list entitled 'the great things about change.'
- Pupils could draw a cartoon that illustrates that a change that we dread can be far worse in anticipation than in reality.

## What about change? (p17)

PURPOSE OF ACTIVITY: to help pupils see the benefits of change.

KEY DISCUSSION POINTS:

- The quotes are saying: change helps you to learn, change keeps things interesting, your attitude towards change has a big impact on how you cope with it, without change you would not feel alive, change makes good things happen, getting good at coping with change will help you to remain positive, always looking back at how things used to be can stop you seeing opportunities... etc.
- To make change sound positive pupils might focus on how change: helps you learn and grow as a person, is exciting, stops you repeating the same things all the time, opens up opportunities, tests you and makes you problem solve... etc.

EXTENSION ACTIVITIES

- Pupils could make a TV advert to go with their poster.
- Pupils could make their own 'changes fact file' where they list changes, how they felt about each one, what they learnt from it and how their life would be now if they had not had that change e.g. moving from infants to juniors, making a new friend, joining a new club, having to do a new chore at home, learning to ride a bike... etc.
- Pupils could discuss what makes some changes a horrible experience e.g. feeling like we had no control over what happened, having no one with whom to talk our worries through, having a lot of change at once, facing a change that makes us spend time doing something we see no point in... etc.

## The effects of peer pressure and influence (p18)

SUPPORTING LEAFLET: Changing relationships (pp 44-45)
PURPOSE OF ACTIVITY: to consider peer pressure and influence and how much it can affect you.

KEY DISCUSSION POINTS:

- Peer pressure and influence can be good or bad. For example, your peers could either try to persuade you to do, or not to do something dangerous. It depends on who your peers are and how they behave.
- It can sometimes take confidence to be different.
- Nobody likes to be teased and most people avoid it. However, you would need to think twice if

avoiding being teased makes you do something you don't want to do.

EXTENSION ACTIVITIES:
- Pupils could role-play a moment of peer influence and/or pressure and show an outcome where they give in to it and an outcome where they resist it.
- Pupils could devise a magazine style advert
  - That would help people be more aware of peer influence and/or pressure.
  - That would help people to have the courage to be different.
  - That shows how peer influence can be a bad thing.
  - That persuades people to think before they succumb to negative peer pressure.

## Peer influence – being 'cool' (p19)

SUPPORTING LEAFLET: Changing relationships (pp 44-45)
PURPOSE OF ACTIVITY: to consider how succumbing to peer influence is not always a 'cool' thing to do.
KEY DISCUSSION POINTS:
- It sometimes takes courage to be different but people usually admire a person that sticks to their guns and only does something because they really want to and not because everyone else is doing it.
- Many adults succumb to peer influence. People like to fit in and being part of a group can make people feel supported. This is great if that group is pursuing positive activities! Excluding someone because they are 'different' is an unpleasant thing to do and can be bullying.

EXTENSION ACTIVITIES
- Pupils could discuss the question, 'What makes someone scared to be different?'
- Pupils could design and draw a poster that does one of the following things:
  - Encourages people to respect everyone as they are: 'cool' or not!
  - Questions whether being 'cool' is really cool!
  - Tells people that what you look like is not the most important thing – personality is what really counts.
  - Tells people it's better to make decisions for yourself than do what everyone else is doing.

## Advice about peer pressure and influence (p20)

SUPPORTING LEAFLET: Changing relationships (pp 44-45)
PURPOSE OF ACTIVITY: to consider how to deal with negative peer pressure and influence.
KEY DISCUSSION POINTS:
- Peer influence is when you do something because everyone else around you is doing it. Joining in makes you feel part of something. Unfortunately, sometimes this can involve being nasty to another person or doing something you don't want to do.
- Peer pressure is when someone your age puts direct pressure on you. This can be done by persuasion, teasing and sometimes by someone insisting forcefully. Direct peer pressure does not happen as often as a person deciding to do something because of peer influence.
- Standing up to peer influence and pressure does sometimes take courage. Most people respect a person who knows their own mind and remains true to themselves.
- Sometimes assertively declaring what you want to do is enough e.g. 'No, I really want to play in the orchestra. I really enjoy it.'
- True friends respect the fact that you might want to do something different.
- Peer pressure and influence can sometimes be positive e.g. if a person persuaded you to try a new club and you really enjoyed it.

EXTENSION ACTIVITIES:
- Pupils can think of things they have done because of peer pressure. Were they sometimes positive experiences?
- Pupils could consider how peer influence and pressure could affect health choices for themselves and others.

## Help (p21)

SUPPORTING LEAFLET: Getting help and support (pp 42-43)
PURPOSE OF THE ACTIVITY: to consider different sources of help, when you might need help and how to access it.
KEY DISCUSSION POINTS:
- Sometimes people see asking for help as a weakness or a failure. Knowing when you need help and how to get it is actually a strength and a skill for life.
- Some reasons why a person might not ask for help are: they don't know who to turn to, they don't believe anyone could actually help, they are scared that they won't be taken seriously or that someone

might think they are making a fuss over nothing, they don't want to look weak or not in control.
- Some things that can help people to ask for help are: lessons/discussion like this, clear signposting of advice and support (helplines, pastoral carers etc), a school culture where pupils are encouraged to ask for help, requests for help being taken seriously… etc.
- Depending on the problem, if people don't ask for help they can be left suffering in silence. This can make them very miserable and stressed.

EXTENSION ACTIVITIES
- Pupils could make a TV advert, a magazine advert or a radio advert that sells the idea that asking for help is a positive thing to do.
- Pupils could discuss the question, 'If you did turn to someone for help, how would you want them to behave?'

## Who would you turn to? (p22)

SUPPORTING LEAFLET: Getting help and support (pp 42-43)
PURPOSE OF ACTIVITY: to consider who pupils would turn to if they needed help and what might stop them from doing so.
KEY DISCUSSION POINTS:
- It is really healthy for everyone to have a support network: different people that we turn to depending on the type of help we need. These people might include a parent/carer, a teacher, a school nurse, a neighbour, a friend, a relative, an adult that runs a club, a doctor… etc.
- Some people ask for help and support more readily than others.
- Some people do not ask for help because: they think asking for help makes them weak, they are scared someone will laugh at their problem, they might think that asking for help is like moaning (which it is not), they are not sure who to turn to… etc.

EXTENSION ACTIVITIES
- Pupils could draw their support network using a metaphor e.g. the people in the support network are the root of a tree, signposts, parts of a smiling face… etc.
- Pupils could role-play persuading someone who is reluctant to tell a teacher that they are being bullied.
- Pupils could role-play a person who is good to get advice from and someone who is awful.

## Anti-bullying (p23)

SUPPORTING LEAFLETS: Getting help and support (pp 42-43), Anti-bullying (pp 46-47)
PURPOSE OF THE ACTIVITY: to revise anti-bullying before pupils go to secondary school.
KEY DISCUSSION POINTS:
PART 1
- If someone calls someone a nasty name once, it is definitely bullying. FALSE – a one-off incident is only bullying if the person felt they could not defend themselves and they were scared it might reoccur.
- Some people deserve to be bullied. FALSE – but sometimes people who have been bullied blame themselves and this makes them less likely to tell an adult.
- If a person is being picked on and feels like they cannot stick up for themselves, they are being bullied. TRUE
- The bully is always bigger than the person they bully. FALSE – it has nothing to do with size. There is always a power imbalance.
- Bullying can make people very miserable, become ill and dread coming to school. TRUE
- Some bullies make people hand over their possessions. TRUE
- Bullying always involves hitting someone. FALSE
- Schools have to know what they are going to do if bullying happens. TRUE – A school must have an anti-bullying policy or clear guidance about how to deal with bullying (e.g. behaviour policy)
- If you see someone being bullied the best thing to do is ignore it. FALSE – to combat bullying everyone needs to feel that it is their responsibility to do something about it.
- Bullying should always be reported. If bullying does not stop, it needs to be reported again. TRUE
- Bullying usually means that a person has been nasty to you more than once. TRUE – bullying nearly always happens repeatedly over a period of time.
- If you are bullied, you need to tell someone and keep telling people until someone makes the bullying stop. TRUE
- Some bullies use mobile phones to bully. It is not a good idea to give your mobile phone number out to everyone. TRUE
- Deliberately ignoring someone and leaving them out can be bullying. TRUE
- Only boys bully. FALSE
- Bullying needs to be taken seriously. TRUE
- Children and young people can ring ChildLine (0800 1111) for advice if they are being bullied or

if they are bullying someone at any time of the day and night and the calls are free. TRUE

PART 2
- The approach a child or young person takes when they witness bullying will depend on each situation. If they feel they can do something about the bullying without putting themselves in danger, then they need to. As a minimum, a witness needs to find an adult to tell.

EXTENSION ACTIVITIES
- Pupils could ask for a copy of the secondary school's Anti-bullying Policy and make a child friendly version (as a poster, leaflet, short play, advert... etc.)
- Pupils could consider all the reasons why a pupil might not report bullying e.g. they are scared someone will not take it seriously, they are scared of repercussion from the bully, they have not recognised that what they are experiencing is bullying, they don't know who to turn to, they think they should be able to sort it out themselves... etc.

# Going to secondary school – how do I feel? (p24)

SUPPORTING LEAFLET: A big change? (pp 40-41)
PURPOSE OF ACTIVITY: to open up discussions about how pupils feel about moving up to secondary school.
KEY DISCUSSION POINTS:
- Pupils might find it hard to decide upon one visual representation of how they feel. If this is the case they could draw a few faces and list the things around each face that make them feel that way.
- A change as big and complex as going to secondary school is likely to cause a mixed bag of emotions – certainly at the anticipation stage.

EXTENSION ACTIVITIES
- The class could collectively list all the things they feel neutral/negative about that could be addressed in subsequent lessons.
- A list of positive things could also be constructed and added to as more activities are completed.

# Feelings about secondary school (p25)

SUPPORTING LEAFLET: A big change? (pp 40-41)
PURPOSE OF ACTIVITY: to explore what causes most anxiety about going to secondary school.
ACTIVITY NOTES: This could be used at the beginning of a block of activities on transition to secondary school and the end to see if attitudes have changed. Ask pupils to complete the sheet individually and then ask them to share their feelings with a friend – if they are happy to do so.

KEY DISCUSSION POINTS:
- When pupils have indicated a negative response to a particular change, further discussion can tease out why pupils feel that way and clarify what their expectations of that particular change is and if it is exaggerated or not.

EXTENSION ACTIVITIES
- Small groups of pupils could take one change at a time and draw a spider diagram (or mind map) to explore the implications of each change.
- Pupils could order the changes from those they perceive to be the biggest to the smallest.

# Getting to know your new teachers (p26)

PURPOSE OF ACTIVITY: for pupils to get used to the idea of having many different teachers.
KEY DISCUSSION POINTS:
- Having lots of different teachers can be interesting. It means you take slightly longer to get to know each one as you have them less frequently than your class teacher at primary school.
- The advantage of having many teachers is that if you don't like a particular teacher, you don't have them all the time.
- Different teachers have different routines, levels of strictness, sense of humour, give different amounts of homework etc. You soon know what you can and cannot get away with!

EXTENSION ACTIVITIES:
- Pupils could draw and label their idea of the ideal secondary school teacher.
- Pupils could discuss attributes of a teacher that they would least like to have at secondary school.

# Secondary school freeze-frames (p27)

PURPOSE OF ACTIVITY: to explore pupils' anxieties towards and understanding of secondary school.
ACTIVITY NOTES: this activity could be done as a starter to gain insight to pupils' views about secondary school or as a finish to a programme of work dedicated to transition to secondary school. Explain to pupils that they must be clear about what each person in the freeze-frame is doing, thinking and feeling as you will take them out of the photo to interview them.
KEY DISCUSSION POINTS:
- It might be interesting to see whether pupils have generally created freeze-frames with a positive or

negative focus.
- Pupils need to consider how realistic they think their freeze-frame is. Challenge any that you consider to be very unlikely.

EXTENSION ACTIVITIES
- Pupils could list three things they learned from doing this activity.
- Pupils could act out the rest of the scene – starting from before and ending after each freeze-frame.

## Transition quiz (p28)

SUPPORTING LEAFLET: A big change? (pp 40-41)
PURPOSE OF ACTIVITY: to take a light-hearted look at the effect of transition to secondary school.
KEY DISCUSSION ISSUES:
- Pupils usually find this an entertaining way of looking at the move up to secondary school.
- The key points the quiz makes about secondary school are: the rumours about heads being flushed down toilets are unfounded, homework is manageable, there is more science equipment, you get help to find your way around, there are specialist teachers, you make new friends, you have a new route to school to get used to, it does not take long to get used to secondary school.

EXTENSION ACTIVITIES:
- Pupils can list the serious points the quiz makes.
- Pupils could make a similar quiz aimed at much younger pupils going from infant to junior school.

## Some information for my secondary school teachers...(p29)

PURPOSE OF ACTIVITY: to consider the information they might want to share with their secondary school teachers and to produce a sheet that could be sent along with them to secondary school.
KEY DISCUSSION POINTS:
- It can be a meaningful activity for pupils to reflect upon their own learning at a time when they are about to go to a new school.
- Going to secondary school can be an opportunity to make a fresh start.

EXTENSION ACTIVITIES:
- Pupils could add more details to the back of their sheets such as: hopes and dreams for the future, what I want to be when I grow up, clubs I would like to join at secondary school... etc.
- Pupils could make a pack for themselves about going to secondary school including activities that they have completed in lessons about moving up to secondary school. They could refer to this pack when they arrive at their new school.

## Turn over a new leaf (p30)

PURPOSE OF ACTIVITY: to consider the transition to secondary school as an opportunity to turn over a new leaf.
KEY DISCUSSION POINTS:
- New starts can be an opportunity to change old habits and behaviours.
- At secondary school, teachers are unlikely to know much about each pupil. This can give pupils the opportunity to make a fresh start – especially if they were often told off in primary school!
- Secondary school is the last bit of your compulsory education and it is where you first get an opportunity to gain some qualifications.

EXTENSION ACTIVITIES
- Pupils might like to think of new leaves they might want to turn over in their home life.
- Pupils could write their hopes and dreams for secondary school.

## A letter to yourself (p31)

PURPOSE OF ACTIVITY: to consider advice pupils could give to themselves to help them to cope with the first few days of secondary school.
KEY DISCUSSION POINTS:
- With any change, time is needed to adjust. During the adjustment period, emotions can be slightly negative – but not always.
- Secondary school pupils often say that after the first week, they feel like they have been at the school for a long time.

EXTENSION ACTIVITIES
- Pupils could consider other times of change in their past and the advice they would have given to themselves.
- Pupils could write the top ten tips for helping settle into secondary school.

# What do the pupils at secondary school say? (p32)

SUPPORTING LEAFLET: A big change? (pp 40-41)
PURPOSE OF ACTIVITY: to consider what pupils say about moving to secondary school and the advice that can be gained from their comments.
KEY DISCUSSION POINTS:
- Clearly every pupil's experiences will be different but many pupils who have recently arrived at secondary school look back upon transition and consider that it was not particularly traumatic.
- As with changes of all kinds, the build-up can be more unnerving than the reality.

EXTENSION ACTIVITIES
- Pupils could compose a list of questions that they would like to have answered by secondary school pupils – if an opportunity to ask such questions can be organised.
- Pupils could brainstorm answers to the question, 'What have I heard about secondary school?'

# How organised are you? (p33)

PURPOSE OF ACTIVITY: to consider personal organisation skills and how developed they are.
KEY DISCUSSION POINTS:
- In the adult population, it is true that some people show more organisational skills than others.
- There are tips that people can follow to help them be more organised: e.g. write lists and plans, try not to leave things until the last minute, always keep things in the same place, practise remembering yourself and don't rely on someone else to remind you, keep a diary and allocate time for completing tasks, allow plenty of time to do things as you cannot always accurately predict how long something will take,… etc

EXTENSION ACTIVITIES
- Pupils could give advice to the character, 'Disorganised Diane' who is always late, has always forgotten to bring what she needs, leaves everything to the last minute, loses everything etc.
- Pupils could set themselves an organisation challenge in response to the activity.

# Road traffic accidents (p34)

PURPOSE OF ACTIVITY: to help pupils consider road safety issues unique to when they first go to secondary school.
KEY DISCUSSION POINTS:
- Quite often shock tactics are used in campaigns like these. However, shocking people is not always the most effective way of getting a message across as people see the sensationalised 'shock' as unrealistic and don't relate it to their own experiences. Some pupils might consider using a more practical message such as 'know your route'.
- Pupils could think of a variety of messages before choosing the one they think will have most impact. The messages might be: familiarise yourself with the route before you start at your new school, paying attention to your friends is more fun than paying attention to road safety – but it keeps you safe/alive, when you first go to secondary school, you are more likely to be involved in a road traffic accident, allow plenty of time to get to school – or if you're late, don't take risks because you are in a hurry.

EXTENSION ACTIVITIES:
- Pupils could develop a teenage-friendly 'green cross code' for secondary school pupils.
- Pupils could consider the route they will take to secondary school and how to keep risk to a minimum.
- Pupils could design a lesson for secondary school pupils to persuade them to take more care when they cross the road.

# To secondary school I go! (pp35-36)

PURPOSE OF ACTIVITY: to consider the idea that anticipating change can cause more worry than the actual reality of change.
KEY DISCUSSION POINTS:
- The story describes an 'anxiety dream'. Quite often, when people are anxious, they have dreams like this.
- This story highlights that when a person feels anxious about something, their anticipation of bad things happening can be exaggerated.
- In this story, the person has biology, physics and Spanish lessons. Many secondary schools teach general science in Year 7 and sometimes languages other than Spanish are taught. This could present an opportunity to talk about the subjects that are taught in Year 7.

EXTENSION ACTIVITIES
- Pupils could make up some more bizarre happenings that would not look out of place in this story.

# Coping with change

Change means that you have to get used to something new. Sometimes change is something you have been looking forward to and sometimes it's something that you have been dreading.

1) Think about the following changes. Would you look forward to them or dread them? Mark each change with:

| D for dread | LF for look forward to | DK for don't know |
|---|---|---|

| | | | |
|---|---|---|---|
| Having a birthday and being one year older. | | Having to do more jobs around the house to get your pocket money. | |
| Moving up to a new year group in primary school. | | Starting a new club after school. | |
| Someone in your class leaving your school and moving away. | | Doing a new sport in PE (one you have never tried before). | |
| Wearing a new coat. | | Starting a new topic in history. | |
| Being given a dinner at home that you have never had before. | | Moving where you sit in class. | |

2) Share with a partner. Would they dread and look forward to the same changes?

3) Discuss with a partner. What do you think makes a person look forward to a change and what makes him or her dread it?

4) Try and order the following changes from the 'biggest' to the 'smallest.'

- a) A new hairstyle
- b) Sitting in a new place in class
- c) Moving to a completely new town
- d) Having a different teacher for a day at primary school
- e) Wearing a new pair of shoes
- f) Moving house in the same town

BIGGEST _____ SMALLEST

5) Discuss with a partner
- What makes a change a small one?
- What makes a change a big one?
- Do you think going to secondary school is a big or a small change? Give a reason for your answer.

16

# What about change?

*A smooth sea never made a skilful mariner.*
Anonymous

*We are like tea bags – we don't know our own strength until we're in hot water.*
Sister Busche

*The only difference between a rut and a grave is their dimensions.*
Ellen Glasgow

*Continuity gives us roots; change gives us branches, letting us stretch and grow and reach new heights.*
Pauline R. Kezer

*Resolve to be a master of change rather than a victim of change.*
Brian Tracy

*If nothing ever changed, there'd be no butterflies.*
Anon

*When one door closes, another opens. But we often look so regretfully upon the closed door that we don't see the one that has opened for us.*
Alexander Graham Bell

*When you are through with changing, you are through.*
Bruce Barton

*Challenges are what make life interesting; overcoming them is what makes life meaningful.*
Joshua J. Marine

*Change always comes bearing gifts.*
Price Pritchett

*Life's challenges are not supposed to paralyse you, they're supposed to help you discover who you are.*
Bernice Johnson Reagon

*If you don't like something change it; if you can't change it, change the way you think about it.*
Mary Engelbreit

*It is not the strongest of the species that survive, nor the most intelligent, but the one most responsive to change.*
Author unknown

*Our only security is our ability to change.*
John Lilly

1) Read through each of the quotes and discuss with a partner what each one is saying about change and challenge.

2) Try and think of a change in your life that brought you good things – even if you dreaded it at first. Share this with your partner.

3) Work with your partner to design and draw a poster that sells 'change'. You will need to make change sound like a fantastic thing so that everyone wants to go and get some. Use some of the good things these quotes say about change to help you.

# The effects of peer pressure and influence

**Peer pressure:** someone persuading you to do something e.g. someone pressurising you to skive off school.

**Peer influence:** doing something because it is what everyone else is doing e.g. wearing trendy clothing.

**Discuss with a partner:**
Do you think peer pressure and influence are always bad?

Now think about how you respond to peer pressure and influence.

Consider how much you agree or disagree with each of the following statements and write the number in the table below.

① STRONGLY AGREE   ② AGREE   ③ UNSURE   ④ DISAGREE   ⑤ STRONGLY DISAGREE

| | |
|---|---|
| I like to feel that I 'fit in' with all of my friends and not stand out too much. | |
| I would smoke if I was being teased because I refused to. | |
| I would do something dangerous if it made me look good. | |
| I only do things that I really want to do. | |
| If a group of people were teasing someone I did not know, I would laugh. | |
| Whether I did something that I did not really want to do would depend on who it was trying to persuade me. | |
| I think that it would be hard to persuade me to do something silly. | |
| I think it is really important that everyone thinks I'm great. | |
| I would do anything to avoid being laughed at by other people. | |
| If someone teased me about the shoes I was wearing, I would never wear them again. | |
| I would have the courage to wear a hideous coat to school! | |

Moving On Up! © Molly Potter 2009

# Peer influence – being 'cool'

When we are children and teenagers we often don't like to be seen as different from everybody else. When we get to secondary school we usually want everyone to think we are 'cool'. We can sometimes be scared to be different in case someone teases us. This can mean we do things that we wouldn't do if we were on our own or just with a close friend.

Being 'cool' is almost like a set of rules that teenagers and children give to themselves. To be 'cool' you have to follow these rules. Aren't there enough rules already?

1) Write a list of rules that you think a person would need to follow to be 'cool'.

Think about:

* clothing
* hairstyle
* shoes
* hobbies and interests
* the way a person has their bedroom or house
* 'cool' parents

* behaviour and attitude at school and outside school
* personality
* friends
* how much like a grown up a person is...

2) Now write a list of rules that the same person would have to follow to be the least cool person in the world!

3) Discuss these two sets of rules: is it really important which set of rules you are closer to following? Are 'cool' people really better than people who are not 'cool' at all?

4) Which of the following do you think makes a person REALLY 'cool'?

| | | |
|---|---|---|
| Always wears the latest fashion. | OR | Wears what they really want to wear whether it's trendy or not. |
| Works hard at school and does well. | OR | Messes about because it makes people laugh. |
| Has parents/carers that give them rules and supports them. | OR | Has parents/carers that let them do whatever they want. |
| Says when they are upset about something. | OR | Never shows emotion. |
| Joins in when someone is being teased. | OR | Sticks up for people. |

5) What do you think can be great about a person who never follows the 'cool' rules?

# Advice about peer pressure and influence

When you go to secondary school, your relationships with your teachers and your friends change. In some ways your friends become more important and you know your teachers less well because you have more teachers and spend less time with each one. This can mean your friends have more influence on you. This can be a good thing but it can also be a bad thing.

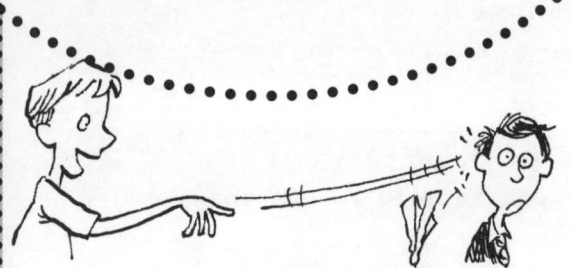

## What advice would you give the following secondary school pupils?

"My friend Gary has started to mess about a lot in lessons. He calls me a swot when I get on with my work. I am sick of him teasing me and I really don't want to get into trouble."
*Eric, Year 7*

"Lots of the pupils in my French lessons have started picking on this boy called Charlie. He's alright but they are always teasing him and calling him names. Last French lesson I joined in but now I feel really bad about it. I think everyone will expect me to carry on joining in because they thought it was really funny."
*Sandeep, Year 7*

"I was nominated to be the year group rep for the school council and I am really pleased. My friend Sam keeps saying that being on the school council is for losers. I really want to be the rep but if Sam keeps on at me I might have to change my mind."
*Ashley, Year 9*

"On my way home from school my friend Olivia keeps trying to persuade me to try a cigarette. I know that I don't want to become a smoker but I also think Olivia won't be my friend anymore if I keep refusing."
*Tansy, Year 8*

"I have just been chosen to play in the school orchestra. I am really pleased about this but my friend Terry says I shouldn't be playing music – I should be trying out for the school football team. He says sport is for boys – not music."
*Pablo, Year 7*

Moving On Up! © Molly Potter 2009

# What to do when you need help

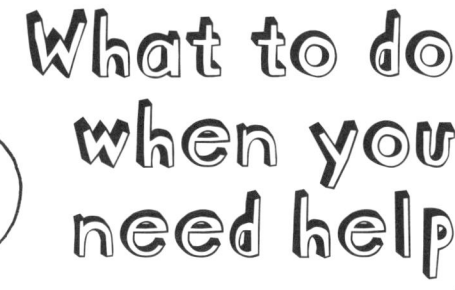

If anyone finds themselves in a situation they do not think they can sort out on their own, they need to find some help. They need to keep looking and asking for help until things are sorted out. This might sometimes mean being quite persistent about finding and getting help.

Some of the kind of things a person might need help with are:

- Bullying
- Feeling self-conscious
- Relationship worries
- Crushes
- Friends
- Medical problems
- Relationships with parents/carers
- Feeling unliked
- Fashion
- Schoolwork
- Homework
- Having arguments
- Feeling left out
- Feeling different
- Having too much to do
- Rules and restrictions
- Feeling depressed
- Feeling stressed
- Growing up
- Coping with change
- Pressure to do things they don't want to do

1) Many adults and young people are not very good at asking for help. List as many things as you can think of that might stop a person from asking for help.

_____
_____

2) What helps a person to ask for help?

_____
_____

3) What kind of things might happen to a person that never gets help?

_____
_____
_____

4) List all the possible sources of help and advice that you can think of. Include different people (friends, teachers, club leaders, neighbours, relatives), professionals and organisations including helplines.

_____
_____
_____

Moving On Up! © Molly Potter 2009

# Who would you turn to?

If something is bothering you and you cannot sort it out, it is really important to find someone who can help you. When you are at secondary school, you might find that you sometimes need help.

## A) Who would you turn to first...

- If you were unhappy about arguments that you were having at home?
  _____
- If you were finding your school work really difficult?
  _____
- If you were worried about something to do with the changes of puberty?
  _____
- If you were being bullied?
  _____
- If you had fallen out with one of your closest friends?
  _____
- If you needed some advice on what to buy someone for their birthday?
  _____
- If you had a crush on someone and it was causing you a lot of upset?
  _____
- If you were worried that you might be ill or that you had something wrong with you?
  _____

## B) Discuss these

1) Which of the following make a person good to turn to for help, support or advice? Which would not?

| Lets you speak without interrupting you. | Laughs and makes out your problem is not that bad really. | Keeps secrets if you ask them to. |
|---|---|---|
| Tells you about a time when they felt the same and makes the conversation all about them – not you. | Takes your worry seriously. | Says sympathetic things such as, 'that must be really difficult for you.' |
| Does not look that interested in what you have to say. | After hearing what your problem is, they tell you what they think you need to do in a bossy way. | Comforts you. |

2) Do you consider yourself to be a person that people find easy to turn to if they need help?

3) What can stop people from asking other people for help?

22

Moving On Up! © Molly Potter 2009

# Anti-bullying

Bullying is one of the most common fears primary school pupils have about secondary school. Although bullying does happen, it is not really common. More people are likely to find themselves being a witness to someone else being bullied.

## 1) Which of the following do you think are true about bullying?

| | | | |
|---|---|---|---|
| Some people deserve to be bullied.<br><br>TRUE/FALSE | The bully is always bigger than the person they bully.<br><br>TRUE/FALSE | Some bullies make people hand over their possessions.<br><br>TRUE/FALSE | Bullying always involves hitting someone.<br><br>TRUE/FALSE |
| If someone calls someone a nasty name once, it is definitely bullying.<br><br>TRUE/FALSE. | Deliberately ignoring someone and leaving them out can be bullying.<br><br>TRUE/FALSE | Schools have to know what they are going to do if bullying happens.<br><br>TRUE/FALSE | Bullying should always be reported. If bullying does not stop, it needs to be reported again.<br><br>TRUE/FALSE |
| Bullying usually means that a person has been nasty to you more than once.<br><br>TRUE/FALSE | Some bullies use mobile phones to bully. It is not a good idea to give your mobile phone number out to everyone.<br><br>TRUE/FALSE | | Bullying can make people very miserable, become ill and really dread coming to school.<br><br>TRUE/FALSE |
| If you are bullied, you need to tell someone and keep telling people until someone makes the bullying stop.<br><br>TRUE/FALSE | Children and young people can ring ChildLine (0800 1111) for advice about what to do if they are being bullied or bullying someone else, at any time of the day and night. The calls are free.<br><br>TRUE/FALSE | | If a person is being picked on and feels like they cannot stick up for themselves, they are being bullied.<br><br>TRUE/FALSE |
| Bullying needs to be taken seriously.<br><br>TRUE/FALSE | Only boys bully.<br><br>TRUE/FALSE | | If you see someone being bullied the best thing to do is ignore it.<br><br>TRUE/FALSE |

## 2) If you saw someone being bullied what are the pros and cons of the following actions that you could take?

* Ignore what is happening.
* Tell the bully to stop what s/he is doing.
* Go and find an adult to tell immediately.
* Join in with the bullying.
* Try to get other pupils nearby to join forces to try and stop the bullying.

# Going to secondary school – how do I feel?

Which of these pictures shows best how you feel about going to secondary school?

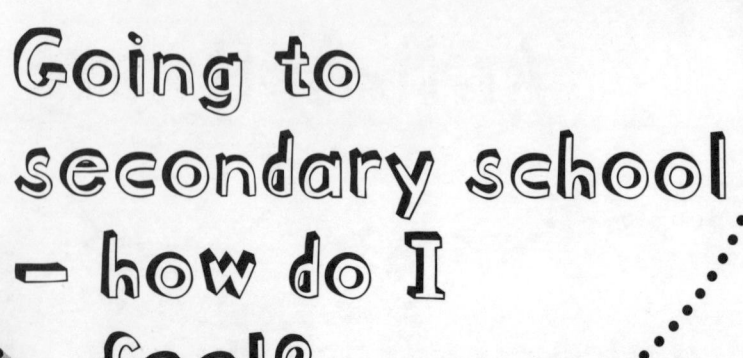
Content

Not bothered

Scared

Confused

Overwhelmed

Excited

Thoughtful

Angry

Draw a picture of yourself in the centre of a piece of paper (it can be a cartoon) that shows best how you feel about going to secondary school. Around the edge of your picture draw and write about all the things you think and feel about going to secondary school.

Moving On Up! © Molly Potter 2009

Put a tick in the boxes that show how you feel about secondary school.

# Feelings about secondary school

|  | OK | Don't like | Excited | Worried | Not sure | No big deal | Great | Sad | Cross | Scared |
|---|---|---|---|---|---|---|---|---|---|---|
| Having more homework | | | | | | | | | | |
| A new journey to school | | | | | | | | | | |
| Having more science and sports equipment | | | | | | | | | | |
| No longer being with all your friends from primary school | | | | | | | | | | |
| Being the youngest in the school | | | | | | | | | | |
| Being put into groups for more subjects | | | | | | | | | | |
| Having lots of different teachers | | | | | | | | | | |
| Being in a much bigger building | | | | | | | | | | |
| Making new friends | | | | | | | | | | |
| More difficult work | | | | | | | | | | |
| Having to look after your possessions in a different way | | | | | | | | | | |
| Having to move to different classrooms for different lessons | | | | | | | | | | |

Moving On Up! © Molly Potter 2009

# Getting to know your new teachers

One thing that will be different about secondary school is that you will have lots more teachers than you had at primary school. This can be interesting! Here are the comments some Year 7 pupils made about their teachers.

Imagine they were your new teachers. Draw a picture (heads only) of what you think they might look like and then consider how you might feel about each one.

**Mrs Jones**

"She's the head of Year 7 and in charge of pastoral care. This means you can go to her if you are worried about anything. I haven't needed to but I reckon she'd be kind if you did. She's sort of firm but fair."

**Mr Johnson**

"He's my maths teacher. He makes lessons really interesting. He is quite strict but he also makes jokes. I think I have got better at maths because of him."

**Mr Chadwick**

"Mr Chadwick is the science teacher. He's nice but perhaps a bit too soft as some people mess about a bit in his lessons but he doesn't seem to mind."

**Dr Purvis**

"She's my science teacher. She's really strict and no one would ever mess around in her lessons. I think she made a joke last week and we weren't sure whether we could laugh or not!"

**Ms Vaudin**

"Miss Vaudin is a new teacher. She teaches French and she is always enthusiastic. Everyone seems to like her and they work hard in her lessons."

**Mr Parkin**

"Mr Parkin is our games teacher. He's quite clearly crazy about all sports. He pushes us quite hard but we enjoy his lessons."

**Mr Baker**

"Mr Baker is my form tutor. He's OK but he makes too many jokes for me to take him seriously! We only have him for 15 minutes every morning."

**Mr Lawrence**

"Mr Lawrence is my art teacher. He's really trendy and cool. Everyone likes him."

### Discuss with a partner:
1) How do you think you will feel about having so many more teachers?
2) What do you think are the good points and the bad points about having lots of different teachers?
3) What type of teacher would you love to have at secondary school?

Moving On Up! © Molly Potter 2009

# Secondary school freeze-frames

A freeze-frame is when everyone stands still in a situation — as if a photograph has just been taken. Work in groups of three and four to produce three of the following secondary school freeze-frames. You only have a title — it's up to you to work out the details!

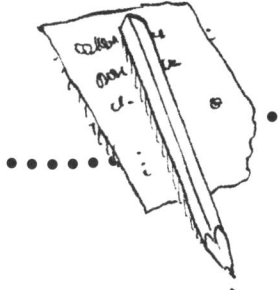

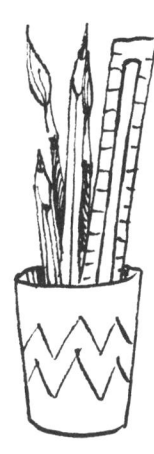

This work is difficult

I did it because everyone else was doing it

The corridor

The misunderstanding

I need help

In trouble with the teacher

Late for a lesson – again!

I just wasn't organised enough

I did really well

Relief!

More homework

Making new friends

Confused!

Getting lost

The big kids

Interesting

Someone lending a helping hand

The science experiment

Brilliant news

The enormous school bag

Good to talk to

# Transition quiz

1. The first time it was reported to kids that they would get their head flushed down the toilet when they went to 'big school' was:
   a) when the dinosaurs were around.
   b) about 1843 – actually we don't know – but our parents certainly had it said to them.
   c) last week.

2. The actual number of children that have had their heads flushed down the toilet since 1843 was:
   a) One – Billy Bolton in 1952 and that's because he was looking for rats.
   b) 87,654 and all at the secondary school you are going to.
   c) We have never heard of it actually happening.

3. The amount of homework you get at secondary school is more than you get at primary school and:
   a) it means you do not have time to sleep any more.
   b) it always has to be completed a minute after the lesson has ended so you have to do it in the corridor.
   c) it is easy to cope with especially if you plan when you are going to do it.

4. When young people are asked about the move to secondary school, one of the things they say is exciting is:
   a) bunsen burners.
   b) the fact that there is no gravity in secondary schools.
   c) being surrounded by taller kids.

5. The fact that a secondary school building is much bigger than a primary school means:
   a) some pupils have been lost inside secondary school grounds until well into their sixties.
   b) you might get a bit lost at first but in less than a week you usually have a good idea about where you are going.
   c) you get fitter.

6. At secondary school, the teachers:
   a) pull the legs off their pupils.
   b) get pupils to clean their cars.
   c) have a greater knowledge of the subjects they teach and that's why you have to have a different teacher for every subject.

7. At secondary school you will:
   a) never be able to speak to another person again.
   b) make lots of new friends.
   c) find lots of farm animals in the corridors.

8. You have more subjects at secondary school than at primary school and this means:
   a) you are more likely to find something you really enjoy and get good at it.
   b) you have many more things to learn e.g. how to make a computer out of an egg box, a piece of string and some sticky tape.
   c) you never know what lesson you are in.

9. Because you have a new journey (and possibly way of travelling) to school you will:
   a) often find yourself accidentally at the seaside.
   b) need to allow plenty of time to get to school until you have got used to the route.
   c) need to keep a portable rocket in your pocket.

10. When adults look back on their secondary school days, they often say:
    a) blimmin' heck.
    b) I found the tea and scones on the lawn delicious.
    c) it was quite different from primary school but I soon got used to it.

Moving On Up! © Molly Potter 2009

# Some information for my secondary school teachers...

Name: _____
Date of birth: _____
Primary school: _____
An interesting fact about me: _____
_____

Most people would describe me as:

careful    tidy    lively    hardworking
kind    imaginative    helpful    interested
responsible    organised    enthusiastic    calm    good at following instructions
good at explaining things    optimistic    fun    polite    friendly    honest

The lessons I like best are: _____
_____

The lessons I like least are: _____
_____

I learn well (tick the things that are true for you):

| | |
|---|---|
| ...in lessons where things are talked about | |
| ...when there are pictures to look at | |
| ...when you actually get to do and practise things | |
| ...when you get time to think about things | |
| ...when you have to draw diagrams | |
| ...when I get to work with friends | |
| ...when it is quiet | |
| ...when you just listen to the teacher | |
| ...when you research things from books | |
| ...when I have to explain things to other people | |
| ...when I can move around the room | |
| ...when there is music playing | |

What I hope to get better at when I get to secondary school: _____
_____

At primary school I got told off (circle what you'd like your secondary teachers to think):

never    hardly ever    sometimes    lots    all the time

Moving On Up! © Molly Potter 2009

# Turn over a new leaf

Starting a new school can be an opportunity to turn over a new leaf. This could mean, for example, if you had not tried very hard in science at primary school, you could be determined to do better at secondary school.

Set yourself three 'new leaves' for secondary school. You could choose from the list below or make up one or two completely new ones.

| New leaf | Tick to choose | Comment |
|---|---|---|
| Try harder in a certain subject (write the subject/s here): | | |
| Be more organised about the stuff I need to take to school | | |
| Get really fit | | |
| Try to do my work more neatly | | |
| Try to fall out with friends less | | |
| Never be late for school | | |
| Worry less about what other people think of me | | |
| Concentrate harder in lessons | | |
| Get told off less! | | |
| Try to be positive about things | | |
| Join at least one club | | |
| Need to be nagged less about getting ready for school in the morning | | |
| Smile more! | | |
| Do homework the day it is set | | |
| **Or some 'new leaves' of your own** | | |
| | | |
| | | |

# A letter to yourself

Going to secondary school is a lot of change in a small amount of time. When anyone has to cope with change, they should expect to feel lots of different emotions while they get used to the new situation. Some emotions to do with change can be negative at first but nearly everyone eventually gets to a point when they feel fine again.

If you were to write a comforting message to yourself that you would receive when you first arrived at secondary school, what would you write?

Dear _____,
I know you have just arrived at secondary school and there are a lot of changes for you to get used to. Here is some advice for you.

Tick the advice that you think will be helpful and then add some more advice:

You might have some negative feelings at first but they will eventually go away. ☐

Soon you will feel like you have been at this school for a long time. ☐

If you do feel worried or sad, talk to someone who you trust, either at school or at home. ☐

You will get used to all the changes. ☐

Remember that all the other new pupils are probably feeling the same as you. ☐

You will soon get into a routine and not have to try so hard to remember what you need to do. ☐

What advice will you give yourself about meeting new people – children, young people and adults?

What advice will you give yourself about getting organised?

What else would you like to say to yourself?

Have a good time!
Best wishes

31

Moving On Up! © Molly Potter 2009

# What do the pupils at secondary school say?

Most people worry about going to secondary school. It is a big change. Here are some comments from pupils who are in their first year of secondary school.

"By about the second week it just feels like school."

"You make new friends very quickly."

"Most of the teachers are really nice. You soon get used to them and their different ways of doing things."

"When I was at primary school I was really worried that I would get lost in such a big school but by the end of the first week you know your way round and it really isn't a problem. The teachers are usually kind about you being a bit late for lessons in the first week."

"Science gets more interesting. You do loads of experiments."

"You do need to be a bit more organised about things like homework and remembering equipment. I have a locker but most of the time I just carry everything around with me in my bag."

"When I was at primary school, I heard lots of rumours about big kids flushing your head down the loo. My mum said that rumour was around when she was a kid. No one has ever heard of it happening. The kids in the years above are OK."

"You can get involved in lots of things that aren't lessons. I am in a drama club and I play hockey for the school. My friend Safi is in the school council."

"You quickly get used to not being at primary school – in fact it quickly seems a long way behind you. I still have good memories of it though."

## What do these pupils say about:

How quickly you settle in? _____

Being worried about secondary school? _____

Getting lost? _____

New friends? _____

The older children? _____

Being organised? _____

Equipment for secondary school? _____

New opportunities? _____

Moving On Up! © Molly Potter 2009

# How organised are you?

There is no doubt that you will need to be more organised when you get to secondary school, and part of growing up is about being more responsible. You will be expected to remember to do your homework and bring it in on time, and bring equipment to school on the right days e.g. PE kit.

How hard or easy you find this will depend on how organised you are. Answer the following questions to find out.

1. When you have homework given to you do you:
   a) Write it into your homework diary with a time when you know you can complete it?
   b) Wait until your mum/dad/carer nags you to complete it?
   c) Go home and do it that night?
   d) Often forget to do it altogether?
   e) Do it but often hand it in late?

2. How do you try to remember people's birthdays?
   a) You don't – you wait until people tell you.
   b) You write them in a diary or on a calendar and always remember them.
   c) Sometimes you remember them.
   d) You have never remembered anyone's birthday.

3. At school do you:
   a) Occasionally need to borrow a pen or pencil?
   b) Lose your pens and pencils all the time?
   c) Always have a pen and pencil?

4. Is your tray or desk at school:
   a) Always messy and full of lots of things that you didn't know you had?
   b) Messy but not so bad that you cannot find anything?
   c) Always tidy?
   d) Mostly tidy?

5. When you are asked to tidy your bedroom do you:
   a) Shove everything under the bed?
   b) Wonder why you have been asked because you always keep it extremely tidy?
   c) Enjoy tidying and sorting things out?
   d) Do everything possible to avoid tidying it?

6. When you leave home for school do you:
   a) Often have to go back because you have forgotten something?
   b) Always have all that you need with you because you packed your bag the night before?
   c) Arrive at school often having forgotten something that you need?

7. If you were asked to list everything you have to remember during the school week would you:
   a) Be able to do this very easily?
   b) Not have a clue because you rely on other people to tell you what you need?
   c) Only know about the things you are interested in e.g. sports kit or art shirt?
   d) Look at the list you have written already?

8. Are you a person who:
   a) Likes to remember and organise things for yourself?
   b) Organises the things that happen each week for yourself but rely on others to remind you about anything new?
   c) Relies completely on your mum/dad/carer to make sure you have all you need?

Now calculate your score and compare it with a friend's. The higher your score, the more organised you are.

| 1. a)5 b)3 c)4 d)0 e)1 | 2. a)2 b)4 c)3 d)0 | 3. a)3 b)0 c)4 | 4. a)0 b)1 c)4 d)3 |
|---|---|---|---|
| 5. a)1 b)4 c)3 d)0 | 6. a)2 b)4 c)0 | 7. a)4 b)1 c)2 d)5 | 8. a)4 b)3 c)1 |

# Road traffic accidents

Children are more likely to be involved in a road traffic accident when they first go to secondary school.

**Possible reasons for this are:**
- The move to school usually means a longer distance is travelled by most pupils.
- The route to secondary school is new to the pupils.
- Sometimes, when secondary school pupils are in groups walking to or from school, they might pay more attention to their friends than potential dangers.
- Pupils might have been allowed to cycle to school for the first time – because of the greater distance.
- Some pupils might take risks to impress their friends.
- Some pupils might travel home in the dark on their own, following an after school club – especially in October after the clocks have gone back.

You have been asked to run a campaign that tries to reduce the number of road traffic accidents with secondary school pupils. You need to produce a poster with a clear message.

Before you start your poster, consider each of the following.

- What else could be done to reduce traffic accidents for secondary school pupils – aside from your poster?
- What will the main message of your campaign be?
- Where would your posters go?
- Which reason or reasons from the list above are you tackling with your campaign?

# To secondary school I go!

I woke up. I will admit that 'I woke up' is only slightly better than, 'Once upon a time' but it's what I did: I woke up. I shuffled to the bathroom, bleary eyed and scratched my head in front of the mirror. I was anticipating the day ahead with a mixture of dread and excitement. Starting at secondary school seemed like an awful lot to get my head round.

Returning to my room, I pulled my new school uniform out of the drawer. At least the uniform meant one less decision to make. I pulled my skirt on, followed by the bright pink and green stripy sweatshirt and noticed that the arms only reached down to my elbows and that lace had been sewn around the neck. I felt pretty sure that this was not what was listed as acceptable wear in the secondary school's prospectus. I floated downstairs to discover that there was no time for breakfast and my mum was panicking about getting the quadruplets and me off to school in time. I ran out of the front door and started my walk to school.

The route was considerably longer than the one to primary school and sometimes my nerves made me feel like I could not walk properly. By the time I entered the school gate, there were crowds of pupils milling around and I did not know a single one of them.

The bell rang. I pulled out the map of the school grounds that I had been given in the last week of primary school. I knew that my form group was 7B and that I was to be registered somewhere in the science block. I looked down at the tatty map in my hand and realised that it was not a map at all, but my mum's shopping list: carrots, tissues, a bike pump, toothpaste, large paddling pool, wheelbarrow and toilet cleaner were not going to help me now. Fortunately, at that point, I saw Brian McFee who I knew was in the same form and followed him into registration. I sat down on an extremely high stool while Mr Green, my form tutor explained the complicated registration procedure involving buttons, codes and passwords. I tried my best to follow them but felt pretty sure by the end of the process that the school would be ringing my mum to ask why I had not arrived.

The walk to my first lesson was hazardous. Pupils, at least double or triple my height and width, barged past me. My bag kept being knocked onto the floor and I had to spend a good ten minutes retrieving the scattered contents of my pencil case from beneath the feet of the surging mob. I was kicking myself for having put a hundred marbles into my pencil case.

Physics, with Mrs Poot, was my first ever secondary school lesson. I sat next to a particularly untalkative boy who seemed to know everyone except me. Mrs Poot welcomed us to Biborough Secondary and launched straight into a lesson on getting a rocket to the moon. She explained that journeying to the moon was to be our homework this week, wrote twenty or so formulae extremely quickly onto the board which she said would help us, and told us to hand in a write-up of our lunar trip by next Monday. Before I could even consider the likelihood of me achieving this task, it was time for English.

Mr Dappletop, our English teacher, was a tiny man that spoke so quietly I could not hear a word he was saying despite being sat right at the front of the classroom. He asked me to hand out copies of a Shakespeare play: 'The Fifth Day Ado About Venice' to everyone and we proceeded to read the play – backwards. To be honest, I would have found it difficult to understand if we had read it forwards. He then set us the homework of copying out the whole play backwards.

Next came games. The sports hall was enormous. I stood there in my fluorescent yellow T-shirt, cycle helmet and wellington boots (everyone else had white T-shirts, black shorts and trainers) and wondered what was in store for us this lesson. The girl next to me turned and whispered, 'It looks like we are going to play Fluzzpin, I love Fluzzpin, we played it all the time at primary school,' as twenty long thin sticks, three hoops, a rope and a parsnip were placed on the floor in front of us. Everyone grabbed a stick and proceeded to play the most complicated game I had ever seen.

After the 'match' the games teacher set us some homework. 'Be sure that you can break the world record for the 100 metres by next Monday – at the latest,' she said as we started to wander towards our next lesson: Biology.

Mr Furrycone, a very enthusiastic teacher, told us as we walked into the laboratory that next week we were to complete an operation where we transplanted the brain of a frog into a tiger and that we would be marked on how successful we had been by how high the tiger leapt after surgery. However, the catch was that the school would only provide the frogs, and that pupils' parents were expected to pay for a tiger per pupil. 'This week,' Mr Furrycone continued, 'however, we will making clothes for the plastic skeleton in the corner and I happen to know he likes clothes that have a floral design.'

The remaining lessons of the day proved to be just as testing and strange. In Spanish I was asked to describe 'my life as a pirate' in Spanish of course, in geography I was asked to mark every single swimming pool onto a globe of the world and in art I was presented with a 10-foot concrete block and a chisel and asked to carve out a sculpture of the Eiffel Tower.

As I left the school gate, my bag packed with homework, I felt unsure of whether I would be able to cope with this every day. When I reached home, I turned to my little sister Gina and noticed that she was playing with a doll in a pink dress. And then it struck me.

'How strange,' I thought, 'Gina hates dolls and the only thing she hates more than dolls is the colour pink. This is a dream.' And despite the fact that every teacher I ever had in primary school told me that a story turning out to be a dream was definitely not clever, it was a dream. But my story doesn't end here.

The following day I did actually go to my new secondary school and do you know what? By comparison, it was a bit boring!

---

1) Sometimes when we are anxious about something in the future we dream about it. What was the first clue that this might be a dream?

2) Underline all the other things in the story that indicate that it is likely to be a dream.

3) What does the story highlight about going to secondary school?

4) Quite often the anticipation and build up to a change causes far more worry than the actual experience of the new situation. If this is true, what advice would you give to a person that was worrying about going to secondary school?

Moving On Up! © Molly Potter 2009

# Photocopiable Leaflets

The following leaflets could be issued to parents/carers and pupils to support the sessions about moving to secondary school that you are delivering. You could encourage pupils to talk through the material on each pupil leaflet with their parents/carers as homework.

## 1) Moving on up – a leaflet for parents/carers

This leaflet outlines all the changes children face when they move up to secondary school. This helps parents/carers to support their child with this process.

## 2) A big change? Moving to secondary school – a leaflet for pupils

This looks at the specific changes and challenges pupils will face when they get to secondary school and gives advice to help them cope.

LESSONS IT COULD BE USED TO SUPPORT:
- Going to secondary school – how do I feel? (p24)
- Feelings about secondary school (p25)
- Transition quiz (p28)
- What do the pupils at secondary school say? (p32)

## 3) Getting help and support – a leaflet for pupils

This leaflet gives guidance about seeking help and support with any problems pupils might face.

LESSONS IT COULD BE USED TO SUPPORT:
- Help (p21)
- Who would you turn to? (p22)
- Anti-bullying (p23)

## 4) Changing relationships – a leaflet for pupils

This leaflet looks at how relationships with teachers and friends can change when pupils move up to secondary school.

LESSONS IT COULD BE USED TO SUPPORT:
- The effects of peer pressure and influence (p18)
- Peer influence – being 'cool' (p19)
- Advice about peer pressure and influence (p20)

## 5) Anti-bullying – a leaflet for pupils

This leaflet gives a summary of the main issues that relate to bullying.

LESSONS IT COULD BE USED TO SUPPORT:
- Anti-bullying (p23)

# Moving On Up

## A leaflet for parents and carers of pupils who will soon be moving to secondary school

- many more pupils than at primary school
- more responsibilities
- a much bigger building
- lots of new friends to make
- different relationships with friends and teachers
- so many different teachers
- lots of different classrooms
- more subjects
- a new route to school
- no more primary school
- being the youngest in the school
- more homework

POP! POP! POP!

## Remember:

Your child has to deal with the move to secondary school around the same time as hormones are starting to fly around their bodies.

Offer support and listen to your child but remember they are likely to start wanting more privacy.

Your child might start to feel painfully self-conscious, wonder if they are 'normal' and become extremely sensitive to what other people say about them. Try to reassure him or her by telling them that nearly everyone experiences these feelings as they grow up.

A natural part of growing up is to want and need to be more independent. You might need to have on-going negotiations with your child about how much freedom you can safely let them have.

At this time, their friends can become very important in their lives. This can make 'fitting in' with peers very important to your child. S/he may listen to friends more than they used to. This can be a good and/or a bad thing. Help your child to understand that they can make decisions for themselves (and not always do the same as their friends) and that they will usually be respected if they remain true to themselves.

Once they arrive at secondary school, many children start to develop strong opinions and become interested in many new things, such as music, fashion, sport... etc. Try to show some interest in the things that start to matter to your child.

Try to appreciate that your child will start to be attracted to other people. Never be tempted to tease your child or belittle the feelings they might have towards other people. You can probably remember just how intense everything felt when you were that age!

Moving On Up © Molly Potter 2009

Moving up to secondary school brings with it a lot of change in a short amount of time. Most children do have some anxiety about these changes. However, every child will have unique worries. One child, for example, might be extremely concerned about the impact on current friendships while another might be really worried about the school work.

Here are a few tips about how to help your child at this potentially difficult time.

1) Find out as much information about your child's new school as you can. It is the 'not knowing' that can cause your child to worry. Details you could find out about might include:
- How much homework will your child get?
- How are lunch times organised?
- What equipment will your child need (e.g. new school uniform, writing equipment, new PE kit)?
- Will your child be grouped with friends from their primary school?
- What clubs does the school run that your child might be interested in?
- Does the school provide pupils with lockers for their personal belongings?
- How does the school help pupils to find their way around the school at first?
- Where can pupils go if they have a problem while they are at school?
- How does the school deal with bullying?

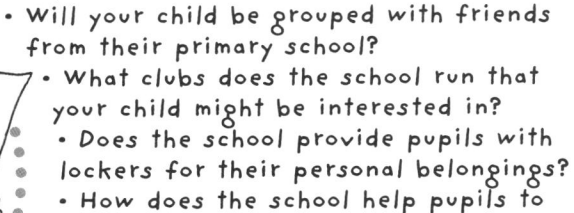

2) Do a practice run of the journey your child will take to their new school. Take care to point out the safest places to cross the roads.

3) See if you can make arrangements for your child to travel to school with another pupil that lives nearby.

4) Help your child to get more organised e.g. write lists of what they need to take to school each day. Encourage your child to pack his/her school bag the night before.

5) Make time to talk and listen to your child during their move to secondary school. It can be obvious when some children are worried but others tend to hide it. Try not to only say 'it will all be all right, don't worry.' Listen to anything they have to say. Advice you could give might include:
- Change always takes getting used to but most pupils say that after a week at a new school, it feels as if they have always been there. In other words the anticipation is nearly always worse than the reality.
- There are definitely things that are worth looking forward to (e.g. making new friends, joining new clubs).

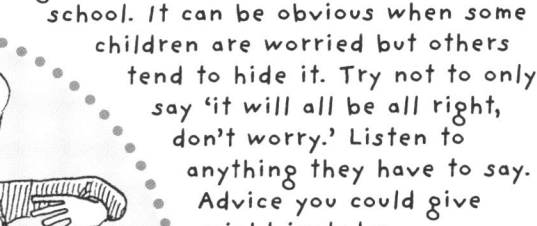

6) Try to make your child feel good about him or herself by discussing what s/he is good at. Also remind your child that no one is brilliant at everything and we all make mistakes. Just give secondary school the best shot you can!

# A big change?

## Moving to secondary school

This leaflet looks at the changes you will encounter when you go to secondary school.

## Get organised

Chances are you will need to be more organised when you get to secondary school. Some people find organising themselves easy but if you don't then you might need some reminders.

- Try and list what you need to take to school each day of the week.
- Try to get into the habit of packing your bag the night before school when things are likely to be less rushed.
- Make a copy of your timetable and put it up somewhere at home.

## Don't get lost!

Nearly everyone at primary school worries about getting lost in their new, much bigger school. Don't worry! You will only be confused for a week at most and most secondary schools put some effort into helping new pupils to find their way around — or forgive them for being a bit late to lessons in the first week.

## New route to school

If you are worried about the new route to school or a new way of getting to school (bus, cycle, walking) then do a practice run before you start for real.

## Don't believe rumours

Untrue stories about heads being flushed down toilets have been around for years and years — don't believe them!

## What's difficult about change?

Some people like change more than others. However, for everyone change means that they have to get used to something new. This can make some people feel a bit unsure or nervous – but usually only for a short while.

Moving to secondary school is a lot of change in a short amount of time. Some of the changes you will look forward to and others you might dread. This is perfectly normal. One thing is for certain, when you have been at secondary school for a week or so, you will already have started to settle in.

## What changes?

The following is a list of changes that happen when a person goes to secondary school. Different people will feel positive or negative about each change:

* Lots of different teachers.
* Friends to make.
* No longer seeing some friends from primary school.
* Moving around the school more between lessons.
* Not having a tray or a desk in one classroom to keep all your stuff in.
* Being put into groups or streams.
* A new route to school.
* A need to be more organised.
* More homework (usually).
* More equipment used in science and sports lessons.
* Being the youngest in the school (after being the oldest).
* A much bigger school to find your way around.
* Work getting more difficult.

## Tips for feeling positive about moving to secondary school

* Very few people would want to stay at primary school until they are 16!
* Change can be very exciting.
* Try to think about all the good things: making new friends, more sports equipment, not being stuck with the same teacher all the time... etc.
* Remember that it really won't be long before you feel like you have always been there.
* Everyone will be feeling the same – even pupils who look really confident.
* If you don't know something, try not to be too shy to ask!
* Talk to friends, family and other people about how you feel if you are worried. This always makes you feel better.

# Getting help and support

**From time to time, everyone has problems...**

I don't feel like I fit in

I am feeling pressurised by so-called friends not to work so hard at school

I have a crush on...

I have fallen out with my good friend

I just can't get all my homework done

I am being bullied

I keep having rows with my parents

I don't feel like my parents understand

The sad truth is that some people believe that asking for help makes you weak in some way. This simply is not true. Knowing yourself and when you need help is something that can make you a very strong person. Bottling things up and failing to ask for help can end up with a person not coping well at all. This usually makes the person extremely stressed and they can end up becoming very ill.

Another sad truth is that some people can feel pressure to always appear to be coping, even when they are not. This can mean they never talk through their worries with another person, which can leave them feeling terrible. It needs to be everyone's responsibility to try and encourage everyone to share their worries and support each other.

**A place you can always turn to whatever the problem is:**

**ChildLine – 0800 IIII**

ChildLine is a FREE helpline for children and young people in the UK. You can call them with any problem – their counsellors are always there to help you sort it out.

ChildLine is open 24 hours a day on every day of the year – so you can ring it ANY TIME.

What's more, there will be no trace of the phone call on your parents' or carers' telephone bill.

Everyone needs help at different times in their lives: children, teenagers and adults. Surprisingly, sometimes the hardest bit is actually recognising that you need help and asking for it.

## Signs that probably mean you need some help:

* Thinking about the same thing all the time.
* Crying a lot.
* Not being able to sleep well.
* Butterflies in your stomach.
* Not feeling like you want to do things you normally love doing.
* Hardly ever feeling safe or happy.
* Feelings of dread.

## Remember:

Everyone has the right to ask for help, however small the problem might seem. If something is bothering you, you need to find someone who can help. Bottling things up will mean that you are unlikely to feel better.

Asking for help shows strength and sense!

## A simple guide to asking for help

1) Make a list of people that you trust and that you would be happy to ask for help. The people in this list will be your 'support network'. This list might include:

* Friends
* A parent/carer
* A neighbour
* A relative – aunt, uncle, grandparent
* A person that runs a club that you go to
* A friend of your mum/dad/carer
* The parent/carer of a friend of yours
* Brothers or sisters
* A teacher
* Other school staff
* A helpline – such as ChildLine (see the back of this sheet)

Your support network will change from time to time.

2) However small the problem might seem, find someone from your list and tell them what is bothering you.

3) If that person does not listen, believe you or support you in a way that helps (this is unlikely but not impossible) find another person from your list and tell them.

4) Keep telling people until you find someone that helps.

5) Remember, sometimes just having someone listen is enough.

# Changing relationships

As you move from primary to secondary school your relationships with the adults in your life and your friends can change.

## Peer influence and pressure

When you get to secondary school, your friends can become more important to you. This can be great. However, sometimes it can make things quite difficult.

Many teenagers want to fit in and be like everyone else. This can make them want to do everything that their friends are doing (e.g. wearing the 'right' clothes) and it can make them a bit scared to be different. Most of the time this is not a problem but if someone is made to feel bad because they feel that they cannot choose to do something different, this can cause a lot of upset.

## Be assertive. Be true to yourself

If you find your friends trying to persuade you to do something you can't do or don't want to do the best thing to do is be assertive.

✗ BE PASSIVE: – GIVE IN

"Come on, let's go round Tony's. Your mum won't mind you being late."

"Oh OK"

✗ BE AGGRESSIVE – SHOUT, HIT PUNCH

"Come on, let's go round Tony's. Your mum won't mind you being late."

"Shut up – you are so bossy."

✓ BE ASSERTIVE – state clearly what you do or do not want to happen without upsetting or annoying the other person

"Come on, let's go round Tony's. Your mum won't mind you being late."

"No I really have got to get home, my mum gets really worried when I am late."

Moving On Up © Molly Potter 2009

## Your teachers

At primary school you have most lessons with one teacher (your class teacher). At secondary school you will have lots of different teachers and therefore you won't know them as well as you knew your primary school teacher. Most pupils have a form or registration tutor and a head of year that will stay with them throughout your time at secondary school. You will probably get to know these teacher/s fairly well and you should be able to turn to them if you need help or support with anything.

## Your friends

Most secondary schools make an effort to put friends together in groups so you are unlikely to arrive in a class where you know no one! However, you are more likely to enjoy secondary school if you expect to make new friends than if you try and stay with your old friends.

Even if nearly everyone in your class at primary school ends up going to the same secondary school as you, it is unlikely that they will all be in every one of your lessons.

Don't worry, good friends from primary school can stay good friends even if they are not in the same classes – especially if they spend time together outside school.

At first you might like to meet up with all your primary school friends at break and lunch times but as time moves on, you will probably find yourself spending more and more time with your new friends.

## Making new friends

It might seem nerve-wracking going to a new school and making completely new friends.

Here are some tips about making friends.

* Try to remember that everyone else is in the same position and probably also feels nervous about making new friends and starting at a new school.

* If you do sit next to a friend from primary school, try to speak to some other people too.

* Try not to be shy about starting up conversations. Nearly everyone likes to make a connection with another person. You could start conversations by asking the other person about their primary school, what they think of this school, what they have liked so far about secondary school... etc.

* Give everyone a chance. Try not to decide things about people from what they look like.

* Just as with adults and with the people in your class at primary school, there will probably be people you don't like as much as others. Don't worry if you don't get on really well with every person you talk to.

# Anti-bullying

Something ALWAYS needs to be done about bullying.

This leaflet briefly outlines the main points about bullying.

## What should happen if I report that I am being bullied?

Every school deals with bullying in a slightly different way. However, whatever does happen should help you to feel safe again. If it does not, you have the right to ask for more help and support until you do feel safe again.

## Here are some ways that schools deal with bullying:

* Keep a record of all bullying that happens.
* Deal directly with the bully — possibly involving his/her parents/carers — to make the bully realise the seriousness of the situation. Many schools give bullies punishments.
* Support the person who has been bullied. Check a couple of weeks and then a few months after the bullying has been dealt with that it has stopped.
* Try to sort out the relationship between the bully and the person they have bullied. Sometimes this might not be the best way of dealing with bullying. A school needs to check with everyone (that has been involved in the bullying) that they do want this to happen.

## A place you can always turn to whatever the problem is:

### ChildLine – 0800 1111

ChildLine is a FREE helpline for children and young people in the UK. You can call them with any problem — their counsellors are always there to help you sort it out. ChildLine receives a lot of calls about bullying.

ChildLine is open 24 hours a day for every day of the year — so you can ring it ANY TIME.

Moving On Up © Molly Potter 2009

## What is bullying?

Bullying is when people are nasty to someone on purpose – usually more than once. The person (or people) being bullied feel like they cannot stick up for themselves.

## How do people bully?

There are lots of different ways that people are bullied. Here are a few examples:

* Name-calling, laughing at and teasing someone.
* Forcing someone to do something they don't want to.
* Picking on someone because they might be different in some way.
* Sending nasty text messages or emails.
* Using computer chat rooms or websites to say nasty things about someone.
* Spreading nasty rumours.
* Deliberately leaving someone out.
* Hitting, kicking or punching.
* Making people hand over their possessions.
* Putting someone deliberately in danger.

## What does it feel like to be bullied?

If nothing is done to stop bullying, a person can feel stressed, miserable and very alone. Bullying is a very serious problem and always needs to be dealt with.

## What can people do about bullying?

Every school has to know what it is going to do to prevent bullying. When a school puts a lot of effort into thinking about anti-bullying they realise that it is best dealt with in more than just one way and gets everyone in the school to consider what to do about bullying.

A school that has really thought through what to do about bullying will have:

* A very clear idea about what must happen if any bullying is discovered and made sure everyone in the school community knows this.
* Helped everyone in the school feel responsible for trying to combat bullying.
* Encouraged everyone to report any bullying they know of – whether they are involved or not.
* Considered about anti-bullying every year.
* Lots of lessons about how to have good relationships.
* Invited parents/carers to think about bullying.

## What can I do if I think I am being bullied?

The whole point about bullying is that the person being bullied feels like they cannot sort it out on their own. This clearly means that if you feel like you might be being bullied, you need to tell an adult you trust. If for some reason that adult does not help, you need to find another adult and tell them. KEEP TELLING until someone does something to help. NEVER suffer alone.

# Transition – is it a big deal?

**None of these thoughts has a positive or negative bias, but how do you imagine each one might make a pupil feel?**

- I just want to be like everyone else. It is really important to me that I fit in.
- The way teachers teach us might be different.
- I want to be able to do more without having to ask my parents' permission all the time.
- Teachers will expect me to be more grown-up and responsible.
- You probably have more to do with your friends than the teachers at secondary school.
- There are lots of other things going on in my life like music, fashion, shopping...
- I'll have to leave much earlier in the morning – my secondary school is quite a long way away.
- The secondary school is a huge building.
- I will be taking the bus to school. I used to walk.
- I am getting really interested in all sorts of issues and have quite strong opinions about things these days.
- I am going to have to learn a new route to school.
- My body is changing.
- I'll be in lots of different groups for different subjects.
- I am not sure if I am like everyone else.
- I am going to have at least ten different teachers. I only had two teachers in Year 6 at primary school.
- I will be leaving my primary school behind.
- I will get more homework.
- I will have to move around between classes.
- I am not sure if there is more bullying at secondary school or not.
- There are so many more pupils at secondary school than primary school.
- I know I will have to be more organised.
- I am beginning to fancy other people.
- I am going from being the oldest in one school to the youngest in the next.
- The work will be different – probably more difficult – and there will be more subjects.
- I will need to make some new friends.
- Some of my friends from primary school are not going to my new school.
- I am getting really interested in all sorts of issues and have quite strong opinions about things these days.